Gamifying Education - How to Engage and Motivate Students Through Games

Quick Reads for Busy Educators

Cheryl Angst

Published by Cheryl Angst, 2023.

GAMIFYING EDUCATION - HOW TO ENGAGE AND MOTIVATE STUDENTS THROUGH GAMES

First edition. April 18, 2023.

ISBN: 979-8223761501

Written by Cheryl Angst.

Also by Cheryl Angst

Quick Reads for Busy Educators
Gamifying Education - How to Engage and Motivate Students Through Games
Unlocking Gamification - Exploring the Impact and Importance in Education
Winning in the Classroom - Using Bartle's Gaming Styles to Empower Learners

Table of Contents

Introduction

I was teaching the same science unit on cells for weeks, and my students were disengaged. I attended a professional development session on gamification in education and decided to try it in my classroom. I introduced a game called "Cell Quest" where students earned points for answering questions about cells. The game was a hit! My students were more focused, motivated, and competitive, answering more questions

correctly than in any previous class. I realized that by adding game elements to my instruction, I could keep my students engaged and improve learning outcomes.

AS EDUCATORS, WE KNOW that engagement and motivation are essential for student success. When students are interested in what they are learning, they are more likely to remember the material, apply it in new situations, and develop a love for learning that can last a lifetime. However, achieving this level of engagement can be challenging, especially when students come to class with different interests, backgrounds, and learning styles.

One approach that has gained popularity in recent years is gamification. Gamification is the use of game elements and mechanics, such as points, badges, and leaderboards, to motivate and engage learners in non-game contexts. By applying game design principles to educational content, we can create learning experiences that are more fun, interactive, and rewarding for students.

But gamification is not just about making learning more enjoyable. It has also been shown to have a positive impact on learning outcomes. Studies have found that gamification can increase student motivation, improve learning retention, and foster a sense of competition and collaboration among learners.

In this book, we will explore how to gamify education effectively. We will cover the key components of gamification, such as game mechanics, player types, and feedback loops. We will also provide practical tips for planning, implementing, and measuring the impact of gamification in the classroom.

Whether you are a classroom teacher, a curriculum developer, or a school administrator, this book will provide you with the tools and strategies you need to gamify education and help your students achieve their full potential. So, let's get started!

Chapter 1: Understanding Gamification

GAMIFICATION IS THE use of game elements and mechanics in non-game contexts, such as education, to motivate and engage learners. But what exactly are these game elements, and how do they work?

In this chapter, we will explore the key components of gamification and how they can be applied to education.

Game Mechanics

Game mechanics are the rules and systems that govern gameplay. Examples of game mechanics include points, badges, leaderboards, and quests. These mechanics are designed to motivate players to engage in the game by providing goals to achieve, rewards to earn, and challenges to overcome. In education, game mechanics can be used to create a sense of achievement and progress for students, as well as to encourage healthy competition and collaboration.

Player Types

Player types refer to the different motivations and preferences that people have when playing games. According to game designer Richard Bartle, there are four main player types: Achievers, Explorers, Socializers, and Killers. Achievers are motivated by achieving goals and earning rewards. Explorers enjoy discovering new things and exploring the game world. Socializers are interested in interacting with other players and building relationships. Killers enjoy competition and conflict. In education, understanding the different player types can help teachers design games and activities that appeal to the diverse interests and motivations of their students.

Feedback Loops

Feedback loops are the mechanisms that provide players with feedback on their progress and performance in the game. Examples of feedback loops include visual indicators, such as progress bars or health meters, and auditory cues, such as sound effects or music. In education, feedback loops can help students track their progress and identify areas for improvement. Feedback loops can also be used to reinforce positive behaviors and motivate students to continue learning.

Game Mechanics: The Key to Engaging Learners in Gamification

Some of my students were struggling to stay engaged in class, so I decided to try incorporating game mechanics like points and badges into our lessons. To my surprise, they became more motivated and enthusiastic about learning. They even started competing with each other to earn more points and badges, creating a sense of friendly competition and camaraderie. It was amazing to see how gamification had transformed their attitudes towards learning.

GAME MECHANICS ARE the core elements that make games fun, engaging, and addictive. When used in education, game mechanics can be a powerful tool to motivate and engage learners, improving their learning outcomes and making education more enjoyable.

Let's explore some of the most common game mechanics and how they can be used in gamification to create effective and engaging learning experiences.

Points

Points are one of the most basic game mechanics, and they serve as a way to measure progress and achievement in a game. Points are awarded for completing tasks, answering questions correctly, or achieving other objectives. In gamification, points can be used to incentivize learners to complete tasks or reach learning objectives, providing a sense of accomplishment and progress.

Badges

Badges are digital icons that represent achievements or milestones in a game. Badges can be earned for completing specific tasks or achieving certain goals. In gamification, badges can be used to reward learners for completing learning modules or mastering a specific skill. Badges can also be used to encourage learners to compete with one another to earn the most badges, creating a sense of friendly competition and camaraderie.

Leaderboards

Leaderboards are lists that rank players based on their scores or achievements. In gamification, leaderboards can be used to encourage learners to compete with one another and to provide a sense of progress and achievement. Leaderboards can also be used to create a sense of community and collaboration among learners, as they work together to climb the ranks.

Quests

Quests are missions or tasks that players must complete in a game. In gamification, quests can be used to guide learners through the learning process, providing a clear path to follow and a sense of progress. Quests can also be used to challenge learners and encourage them to think creatively and critically.

Challenges

Challenges are obstacles or barriers that players must overcome in a game. In gamification, challenges can be used to simulate real-world situations and encourage learners to problem-solve and think critically. Challenges can also be used to create a sense of achievement and progress, as learners overcome obstacles and achieve their goals.

Rewards

Rewards are incentives that players receive for completing tasks or achieving goals in a game. In gamification, rewards can be used to motivate learners and provide a sense of accomplishment. Rewards can be in the form of virtual goods, such as digital badges or points, or real-world incentives, such as extra credit, fictional funds to spend in a classroom economy, or tangible prizes.

Game mechanics are the building blocks of gamification, and they can be used to create engaging and effective learning experiences. By incorporating game mechanics such as points, badges, leaderboards, quests, challenges, and rewards, educators can motivate learners to achieve their learning objectives and improve their learning outcomes. With the right game mechanics, gamification can make learning more enjoyable, engaging, and effective.

Understanding Player Types: How to Engage Different Learners in Gamification

I realized early on in my career that not all students learn the same way. I started incorporating gamification in my lessons and discovered the importance of understanding player types. One of my students was struggling to stay motivated, so I decided to try engaging him through social elements. I created a leaderboard that allowed him to see how his progress compared to others, and he became more motivated to participate in class discussions and activities. Another student was motivated by solving puzzles, so I incorporated more quests and challenges into our lessons to cater to his explorer player type. By understanding my students' different player types and incorporating gamification elements that catered to their motivations, I was able to create a more engaging and effective learning experience for all of my students.

IN GAMIFICATION, IT'S important to understand the different types of players or learners and their individual preferences and motivations. By understanding player types, educators can create personalized and engaging learning experiences that cater to the needs and interests of each learner.

Richard Bartle defined four player types, but we're going to look at six. While the last two can be viewed as variations of the others, they are also worth considering as separate types due to their increasing presence in classrooms.

Achievers

Achievers are motivated by progress and achieving goals. They enjoy completing tasks, earning points and rewards, and competing with others. In gamification, achievers can be engaged by setting clear objectives and offering rewards and recognition for their achievements.

Explorers

Explorers are motivated by curiosity and discovery. They enjoy exploring new ideas and concepts, discovering hidden information, and solving puzzles. In gamification, explorers can be engaged by providing them with challenges and quests that require them to explore and experiment with new concepts.

Socializers

Socializers are motivated by social interaction and collaboration. They enjoy working with others, sharing ideas and experiences, and building relationships. In gamification, socializers can be engaged by incorporating social elements like leaderboards, team challenges, and discussion forums.

Killers

Killers are motivated by competition and the desire to win. They enjoy defeating others and coming out on top. In gamification, killers can be engaged by incorporating competitive elements like leaderboards, challenges, and rankings.

Daredevils

Daredevils are motivated by taking risks and pushing boundaries. They enjoy taking on difficult challenges and testing their limits. In gamification, daredevils can be engaged by providing them with challenges that require risk-taking and experimentation.

Strategists

Strategists are motivated by planning and problem-solving. They enjoy analyzing information, developing strategies, and finding solutions to complex problems. In gamification, strategists can be engaged by providing them with challenging puzzles and quests that require strategic thinking and problem-solving skills.

By understanding these player types and their motivations, educators can tailor their gamification strategies to engage each learner in a personalized and effective way. This not only increases engagement and motivation, but also helps learners to develop valuable skills and knowledge that will benefit them in their future academic and professional endeavors.

Player types are a crucial aspect of gamification and understanding them can help educators to create engaging and effective learning experiences. By incorporating elements that cater to each player type, educators can increase engagement, motivation, and learning outcomes. With the right approach to gamification, learners can have fun while developing important skills and knowledge that will benefit them in the long run.

Feedback Loops: How to Use Feedback to Improve Learning and Engagement in Gamification

―――

I remember when I first introduced feedback loops into my classroom using gamification. One of my students, John, was struggling to keep up with the rest of the class. He had been disengaged and was failing to complete his assignments. I decided to introduce a feedback loop by setting achievable goals for him and providing him with feedback on his progress. I gave him regular updates on how he was doing and what he needed to improve on.

Within a few weeks, John's attitude had changed completely. He was more motivated and engaged, and he started to show a real interest in the subject. He even began to set his own goals and look for ways to improve his performance. By using feedback loops, I was able to help John understand his strengths and weaknesses and adjust his learning strategies to achieve his goals. It was a great feeling to see how much he had improved and how much more confident he had become in his abilities.

―――

IN GAMIFICATION, FEEDBACK loops are an essential component that allows learners to receive information about their progress and performance. By providing learners with timely and constructive feedback, educators can help them to understand their strengths and weaknesses, adjust their strategies, and improve their overall learning outcomes.

There are four stages of a feedback loop in gamification:

Goal Setting

The first stage of a feedback loop is goal setting. In gamification, learners need to have clear goals and objectives that they can work towards. These goals can be short-term or long-term and should be achievable and challenging.

Feedback

The second stage is feedback. In gamification, learners need to receive timely and constructive feedback that helps them to understand their progress and performance. Feedback can be provided through various means such as badges, points, leaderboards, and comments from teachers or peers.

Assessment

The third stage is assessment. In gamification, learners need to assess their progress and performance against the goals and objectives set in the first stage. This assessment helps them to understand their strengths and weaknesses and identify areas for improvement.

Adjustment

The fourth stage is adjustment. In gamification, learners need to adjust their strategies and actions based on the feedback and assessment they receive. This adjustment helps them to improve their learning outcomes and achieve their goals.

By incorporating feedback loops into gamification, educators can improve engagement, motivation, and learning outcomes. Feedback loops allow learners to understand their progress and performance, adjust their strategies, and improve their overall learning outcomes.

Feedback loops are an essential component of gamification and can help educators to create engaging and effective learning experiences. By providing learners with timely and constructive feedback, educators can help them to understand their progress and performance, adjust their strategies, and improve their overall learning outcomes. With the right approach to gamification and feedback loops, learners can have fun while developing important skills and knowledge that will benefit them in the long run.

In this chapter, we explored the key components of gamification and how they can be applied to education. By understanding these components, educators can design effective gamified learning experiences that engage and motivate students to learn. In the next chapter, we will explore how to plan and implement gamification in the classroom.

Chapter 2: Planning for Gamification

BEFORE YOU START INCORPORATING gamification into your classroom, it's important to plan and prepare. In this chapter, we'll explore in detail the steps you need to take to effectively plan for gamification in your classroom.

Step 1: Define Your Objectives

The first step in planning for gamification is to define your objectives. What do you want your students to achieve through gamification? Do you want to increase their engagement, motivation, or learning outcomes? Be specific about your objectives so you can create a plan that aligns with your goals.

Step 2: Identify Your Audience

The second step is to identify your audience. Who are your students, and what are their interests and motivations? Understanding your audience is critical to creating a gamification plan that will engage and motivate them.

Step 3: Choose Your Game Mechanics

The third step is to choose your game mechanics. Game mechanics are the rules and elements that make up your gamification plan. Examples of game mechanics include points, badges, leaderboards, and challenges. Choose the game mechanics that align with your objectives and will appeal to your audience.

Step 4: Plan Your Content

The fourth step is to plan your content. What activities, assessments, or lessons will you incorporate into your gamification plan? How will you use game mechanics to reinforce your content and keep your students engaged?

Step 5: Test and Refine

The final step is to test and refine your gamification plan. Try it out with a small group of students and gather feedback. Analyze the data and use it to refine your plan, making adjustments where necessary.

Step 1: Define Your Objectives

Last semester, I decided to incorporate gamification into my English class. I was excited about the potential of using game elements to increase student engagement and motivation, but I realized I needed to define my objectives first.

I started by brainstorming a list of what I wanted my students to achieve through gamification. Then, I narrowed it down to three key objectives that aligned with my teaching goals and my students' interests: increase student participation in class discussions, improve student writing skills, and increase student motivation to read and analyze literature.

To achieve my objectives, I designed a gamification plan that included a points system for participation, a writing challenge with peer feedback, and a literary analysis game with rewards for top performers.

By defining my objectives and incorporating game elements that aligned with those objectives, I saw a significant increase in student engagement, motivation, and learning outcomes. It was exciting to see how gamification could enhance my teaching and help my students achieve their goals.

GAMIFICATION CAN BE a powerful tool for increasing student engagement, motivation, and learning outcomes in the classroom. However, to effectively incorporate gamification into your teaching, it's important to start with a clear set of objectives. In this section, we'll explore step 1 of planning for gamification: defining your objectives.

Why Define Objectives?

Defining your objectives is critical to creating a successful gamification plan. Without clear objectives, it's difficult to design a plan that aligns with your goals and meets the needs of your students. Defining your objectives also helps you measure the effectiveness of your gamification plan and make adjustments as needed.

Tips for Defining Objectives

Here are some tips for defining your objectives when planning for gamification:

- **<u>Be Specific:</u>** Start by defining specific objectives that are measurable and achievable. For example, instead of saying "I want to increase student engagement," try "I want to increase student participation in class discussions by 50%."

- **<u>Consider Your Goals:</u>** Your objectives should align with your overall teaching goals. What do you want your students to achieve in your class, and how can gamification help you get there? Be sure to consider your curriculum and learning outcomes when defining your objectives.

- **<u>Involve Your Students:</u>** Your objectives should also reflect the interests and motivations of your students. Ask them what they want to achieve through gamification and incorporate their ideas into your objectives.

- **<u>Keep it Simple:</u>** Try to limit your objectives to 3-5 key areas. Too many objectives can make it difficult to design a focused and effective gamification plan.

Examples of Objectives

Here are some examples of objectives for gamification in the classroom:

- Increase student participation in class discussions by 50%.
- Improve student retention of key concepts by incorporating game-based review activities.
- Increase student motivation by incorporating a leaderboard and rewards system.
- Encourage teamwork and collaboration by incorporating group challenges and activities.
- Increase student self-reflection and metacognition by incorporating self-assessment activities with immediate feedback.

Defining your objectives is the first step in planning for gamification in the classroom. By setting specific, measurable, and achievable objectives that align with your goals, curriculum, and student interests, you can create a gamification plan that is focused and effective. Remember to involve your students in the process and keep it simple by limiting your objectives to a few key areas. With clear objectives, you can effectively incorporate gamification into your teaching and create a more engaging and effective learning experience for your students.

Step 2: Identify Your Audience

After attending a professional development workshop on gamification, I decided to gamify my math class to increase student engagement and motivation. However, I realized that I needed to identify my audience first.

To do this, I surveyed my students to find out what types of games they enjoyed and what motivated them. I found that many of my students enjoyed games with competition, as well as games that allowed them to progress at their own pace. I also found that some of my students had limited experience with games.

With this information, I designed game elements that catered to my students' interests and motivations. For example, I created a game that involved solving math problems against a clock and competing with other students to get the highest score. I also designed another game that allowed students to progress through levels at their own pace, earning points and rewards for completing each level.

As a result, I saw a significant increase in student engagement and motivation in my math class. By identifying my audience and designing game elements that aligned with their interests and motivations, I was able to create a gamification plan that resonated with my students and improved their learning outcomes.

WHEN DESIGNING A GAMIFICATION plan, it's important to consider who your audience is. Identifying your audience can help you tailor your game elements to their interests, motivations, and learning styles. Here are some tips on how to identify your audience:

Understand Their Age and Background

Different age groups have different preferences when it comes to games. For example, younger students may be more attracted to colorful graphics and sounds, while older students may prefer more complex game mechanics. Additionally, students from different cultural backgrounds may have varying levels of familiarity with games.

Consider Their Learning Style

Students have different learning styles, including visual, auditory, and kinesthetic. Design game elements that cater to their preferred learning style to increase engagement and motivation.

Understand Their Motivation

Students are motivated by different things, such as competition, recognition, or mastery. Identify what motivates your students and design game elements that align with their interests.

Consider Their Prior Knowledge and Experience

Students may have different levels of prior knowledge and experience with games. Design game elements that are accessible to all students, regardless of their prior experience with games.

Get Feedback From Your Students

Ask your students for feedback on your gamification plan. Use their feedback to make adjustments that better align with their interests, motivations, and learning styles.

By identifying your audience and designing game elements that cater to their interests, motivations, and learning styles, you can create a more engaging and effective gamification plan. So, take the time to get to know your audience and design game elements that will resonate with them.

Step 3: Choose Your Game Mechanics

When I was planning my gamification strategy for my English class, I knew that I needed to choose the right game mechanics to engage my students. I wanted to make sure that the mechanics I chose would support my learning objectives and cater to my students' interests.

To choose my game mechanics, I considered the different elements that could motivate and engage my students. For example, I knew that my students enjoyed competition, so I decided to use a leaderboard mechanic to track their progress and create a sense of competition in the class.

I also wanted to encourage collaboration among my students, so I used a team-based challenge mechanic. I split my class into teams and assigned them a challenge to complete, such as creating a group project or writing a collaborative story. This mechanic not only encouraged collaboration but also helped improve their communication skills.

In addition to these mechanics, I also used points and badges to motivate my students to complete assignments and participate in class discussions. This helped to create a sense of accomplishment and recognition for their efforts.

By carefully choosing my game mechanics and making sure they aligned with my objectives and catered to my students' interests, I was able to create a gamification plan that kept my students engaged and motivated throughout the semester.

GAME MECHANICS ARE the building blocks of a gamification plan. They are the rules and systems that define how the game is played, and they can be used to motivate and engage students.

Here are some tips on how to choose your game mechanics:

Consider Your Objectives

Your game mechanics should align with your learning objectives. If your objective is to improve collaboration, for example, you may want to use mechanics such as team-based challenges or shared goals.

Think About Your Audience

Choose game mechanics that cater to your students' interests, motivations, and learning styles. For example, if your students are visual learners, you may want to use game mechanics that involve graphics and images.

Choose Mechanics That Fit Your Content

Your game mechanics should support your content and subject matter. For example, if you're teaching science, you may want to use game mechanics that involve experimentation or exploration.

Use A Variety Of Mechanics

Using a variety of game mechanics can help keep your students engaged and motivated. Consider using mechanics such as points, badges, leaderboards, challenges, and quests.

Make Sure Your Mechanics Are Easy To Understand

Your game mechanics should be easy to understand and follow. If your mechanics are too complex, they may confuse or frustrate your students.

By choosing game mechanics that align with your objectives, audience, content, and are easy to understand, you can create a more engaging and effective gamification plan. So take the time to consider your game mechanics and choose those that will motivate and engage your students.

Step 4: Plan Your Content

As an elementary school teacher, I was excited to incorporate gamification into my lessons to make learning more engaging and fun for my students. However, before I could choose the game mechanics or plan the points system, I had to decide on the content I wanted to teach.

I took some time to reflect on the curriculum and the learning objectives I wanted to achieve. I then brainstormed ideas for how to present the material in a more interactive and engaging way. For example, when teaching about fractions, I decided to incorporate a game where students had to build and combine different fraction blocks to create a whole.

Once I had a solid plan for the content, I was able to think more critically about the game mechanics I wanted to use to enhance the learning experience. I chose game mechanics that complemented the content, such as awarding points for correctly solving fraction problems, and providing bonuses for students who could create the whole fraction the fastest.

By planning my content first, I was able to ensure that the gamification element enhanced the learning experience, rather than detracting from it. The result was a fun and engaging classroom environment that helped my students learn and retain the material in a more effective way.

ONCE YOU HAVE IDENTIFIED your students' needs and interests, it's time to plan your content. Your content should be designed to support your learning objectives and engage your students in a meaningful way.

Map Out Your Curriculum

Start by mapping out your curriculum and identifying the topics and concepts that you want to cover. This will help you create a plan for how to integrate game mechanics into your lessons.

Create Challenges and Quests

Create challenges and quests that align with your learning objectives. For example, if you're teaching history, you could create a quest where students have to research and present on a historical figure or event.

Use Storytelling

Use storytelling to make your content more engaging and memorable. You can create a story or narrative that runs throughout your gamification plan, with each lesson building on the previous one.

Incorporate Multimedia

Incorporate multimedia elements, such as videos and images, to make your content more engaging and interactive. You can also use these elements to provide additional information and context for your lessons.

Provide Feedback

Provide feedback to your students throughout the gamification plan. This can be in the form of points, badges, or comments, and can help motivate students to continue learning and participating in the game.

By planning your content carefully and incorporating game mechanics that support your learning objectives, you can create a gamification plan that engages and motivates your students. So take the time to map out your curriculum, create challenges and quests, use storytelling, incorporate multimedia, and provide feedback to create a truly engaging and effective gamification plan.

Step 5: Revise and Refine

———

I've always wanted to find a way to motivate my students to participate in class discussions and ask questions. I struggled with student engagement until I decided to try incorporating a gamification element into my lessons, using a points system to reward students for participation.

At the beginning of the semester, I introduced the game and explained the rules. Students could earn points by asking questions, answering questions, and contributing to class discussions. I also included bonus points for students who went above and beyond, such as doing additional research on a topic and sharing their findings with the class.

As the semester progressed, I could see a noticeable increase in student participation. Even the shyest students were raising their hands and contributing to discussions. And because I was providing immediate feedback in the form of points, students were motivated to continue participating and engaging with the material.

By the end of the semester, the students were more engaged and motivated than ever before. The gamification element had made a real difference in the classroom, and I knew I had found a powerful tool for motivating and engaging my students.

———

ONCE YOU'VE IMPLEMENTED your gamification plan, it's important to evaluate its effectiveness and make any necessary adjustments. This is where Step 5, revise and refine, comes into play.

Collect Feedback

The first step in revising and refining is to collect feedback from your students. This can be done through surveys, focus groups, or one-on-one conversations. Find out what they liked about the gamification element, what they didn't like, and any suggestions they have for improvement.

Analyze Data

In addition to collecting feedback, analyze data to see how well the gamification element is working. Look at how many points students are earning, how often they're participating, and how well they're performing on assessments. Use this data to identify areas where the gamification element is succeeding and where it needs improvement.

Make Adjustments

Based on the feedback and data you've collected, make adjustments to your gamification plan. This could mean changing the game mechanics, adjusting the points system, or modifying the content to better align with the gamification element. Be sure to communicate any changes to your students, so they understand what's happening and why.

Continue to Monitor

Even after you've made adjustments, it's important to continue monitoring the effectiveness of your gamification plan. Collect ongoing feedback from your students, and analyze data to ensure the changes you've made are having the intended effect. If you find that something isn't working, don't be afraid to make additional adjustments.

By revising and refining your gamification plan, you can create a more effective and engaging learning experience for your students. Remember, gamification is a process, and it takes time to perfect. Keep evaluating and refining your approach, and you'll continue to see positive results in your classroom.

Planning for gamification is critical to creating a successful and engaging learning experience for your students. By defining your objectives, identifying your audience, choosing your game mechanics, planning your content, and testing and refining, you can create a gamification plan that aligns with your goals and meets the needs of your students. With careful planning and preparation, gamification can be a powerful tool to increase engagement, motivation, and learning outcomes in your classroom.

Chapter 3: Implementing Gamification in the Classroom

NOW THAT YOU'VE PLANNED your gamification strategy, it's time to implement it in the classroom. Here are some key steps to follow to ensure a successful implementation:

Introduce The Concept

Start by introducing the concept of gamification to your students. Explain the game mechanics, how points will be earned, and what rewards will be given. Make sure your students understand how gamification fits into the overall learning objectives of the class.

Set Clear Expectations

To ensure that the gamification element runs smoothly, set clear expectations for your students. Outline the rules for earning points, how points will be tracked, and how rewards will be distributed. Be sure to communicate these expectations in a clear and concise manner.

Provide Regular Feedback

One of the key benefits of gamification is the opportunity to provide regular feedback to students. Use the points system to provide ongoing feedback on student progress, and provide additional feedback as needed to help students improve.

Celebrate Successes

Celebrate student successes by recognizing students who have earned a significant number of points or who have achieved specific goals. This recognition can be done in the form of in-class recognition, such as a shout-out or a certificate, or more tangible rewards such as small prizes or extra credit.

Adjust as Needed

Finally, be prepared to adjust your gamification strategy as needed. Monitor student progress and feedback, and make adjustments to the game mechanics or rewards as necessary to ensure maximum engagement and success.

Introduce the Concept

Despite being passionate about science, I was struggling to find ways to engage my middle school students in a unit on the human body. I decided to try implementing gamification, but I knew that I had to introduce the concept in a way that would make sense to them.

I started the class by explaining that we were going to play a game where they would earn points for completing various activities related to the human body, such as labeling organs and describing their functions. I also showed them a leaderboard that would display their progress and the rewards they could earn for reaching certain milestones.

To my surprise, my students were instantly hooked on the game. They were excited to earn points and compete with each other for the top spot on the leaderboard. I could see their motivation and engagement increase as they worked through the activities and achieved their goals.

By introducing the concept of gamification in a clear and engaging way, I was able to create a positive and rewarding classroom experience that helped my students learn and understand the human body.

WHEN APPLIED IN THE classroom, gamification can improve student motivation, increase engagement, and foster a positive learning experience. However, before implementing gamification in your classroom, it is essential to introduce the concept to your students.

Start With An Explanation

Begin by defining gamification to your students. Explain how it can make learning more fun and engaging by incorporating game mechanics such as points, badges, and leaderboards.

Provide Context

Provide context on how gamification can help students learn better. For instance, you can explain how points can serve as an indicator of progress and motivate students to work harder towards a goal.

Explain The Rules

Explain the rules and mechanics of the game to your students. For instance, clarify how points are earned, how rewards are distributed, and how leaderboards work. This information will help students understand how to participate and what is expected of them.

Emphasize Learning Objectives

Emphasize how gamification aligns with your learning objectives. This will help students see how gamification fits into the broader learning experience and encourage them to participate.

Model Gameplay

Finally, model gameplay for your students. Provide examples of how to earn points, how to interact with the game, and how to track progress. This can help students understand the game mechanics and feel more confident in participating.

By following these steps, you can introduce the concept of gamification to your students in a way that is engaging and clear. Introducing gamification can be a powerful tool to create a positive and engaging classroom experience, and can help students become more motivated and invested in their own learning.

Set Clear Expectations

As an Honors English teacher, I wanted to use gamification to motivate my high school students to read more books. However, I knew that I had to set clear expectations to make sure they understood the rules of the game and what was expected of them.

Before starting the game, I explained to my class how it would work and what they needed to do to earn points. I showed them a chart that listed the point values for different types of books, such as classics or non-fiction, and the rewards they could earn for reaching certain point levels.

I also made it clear that the game was optional and that they could still participate in class discussions and assignments even if they didn't want to play. I emphasized that the game was meant to be a fun way to encourage reading and not a requirement for the class.

Thanks to setting clear expectations, my students were able to understand the rules of the game and participate in a way that was comfortable for them. I could see their enthusiasm for reading grow as they worked towards earning points and achieving their goals.

GAMIFICATION CAN BE a powerful tool to create a positive and engaging classroom experience, but it requires careful planning and execution. One crucial step is setting clear expectations for your students. By setting clear expectations, you can ensure that your students understand the rules and mechanics of the game, as well as their role and responsibilities within it.

Define The Rules

Clearly define the rules of the game, including how points are earned, how rewards are distributed, and how the leaderboard works. Be specific and make sure that your students understand the mechanics of the game.

Explain The Rewards

Explain the rewards that students can earn through the game. This can include tangible rewards such as prizes, as well as intangible rewards such as recognition and praise.

Set Clear Goals

Set clear goals for your students to achieve, and explain how these goals align with your learning objectives. This can help students understand the purpose of the game and what they need to do to succeed.

Clarify Roles

Clarify the roles of each student in the game, and explain how they can work together to achieve the goals. This can help create a sense of community and collaboration among your students.

Define Consequences

Finally, define the consequences for not meeting the expectations of the game. This can include losing points or missing out on rewards. Be clear and consistent in enforcing consequences.

By setting clear expectations for your students, you can ensure that they understand the rules and mechanics of the game, as well as their role and responsibilities within it. This can help create a positive and engaging classroom experience that motivates and inspires your students to learn.

Provide Regular Feedback

I wanted to introduce gamification in my pre-calculus class to help my students understand complex concepts more easily. I chose a few game mechanics to incorporate into my lessons and started implementing them in my classroom. I provided regular feedback to my students on their progress and performance, making sure to highlight areas where they were doing well and areas that needed improvement.

One student in particular, Alex, had always struggled with math and was often disengaged in class. However, after introducing gamification and providing regular feedback, I noticed a significant improvement in Alex's participation and performance. He was motivated to earn points and badges in the game, and he worked harder to understand the material so he could do well in the game.

I continued to provide feedback on Alex's progress, offering specific praise for his improvements and suggestions for areas where he could improve further. This ongoing feedback helped Alex stay engaged and motivated throughout the semester, and he ultimately achieved a level of success in math that he had never thought possible.

PROVIDING REGULAR FEEDBACK is crucial when implementing gamification in the classroom. Feedback helps students understand their progress and motivates them to keep playing the game. In this section, we will explore the importance of regular feedback and how to provide it effectively.

Why Provide Regular Feedback?

Regular feedback helps students stay engaged in the game and gives them a sense of accomplishment as they progress. It also helps them understand what they are doing well and where they need to improve. When students receive feedback, they can adjust their behavior and work towards achieving their goals.

How to Provide Effective Feedback?

- **Be Timely:** Provide feedback as soon as possible after a task is completed. This allows students to make adjustments while the task is still fresh in their minds.

- **Be Specific:** Provide specific feedback that highlights what the student did well and what they can improve on. Avoid vague comments such as "good job" or "needs improvement".

- **Be Constructive:** Feedback should be constructive, not critical. Instead of pointing out flaws, provide suggestions for improvement.

- **Use Multiple Formats:** Provide feedback in different formats such as verbal, written, or visual. This allows students to receive feedback in a way that is most helpful to them.

- **Personalize Feedback:** Provide feedback that is specific to each student. This shows that you are paying attention to their individual progress and that you care about their success.

By providing regular feedback, you can create a positive and supportive environment that encourages students to continue playing the game and striving towards their goals. It can also help students develop important skills such as self-reflection and self-improvement.

In conclusion, providing regular feedback is a critical component of gamification in the classroom. By following the tips above, you can provide effective feedback that helps students stay engaged and motivated to achieve their goals.

Celebrate Successes

I've always loved to see my students grow and learn, but I wanted to make the process even more enjoyable and engaging for them. That's why I decided to gamify my classroom and introduce various game mechanics to my lessons.

At first, some students were hesitant about the idea, but they soon became excited about the challenges and rewards that were involved. They worked hard to earn points and level up, and it was a pleasure to see them grow in confidence and knowledge.

One day, a student who had struggled with a particular topic for weeks finally achieved a breakthrough and understood the concept. I could see the pride in their eyes and how much it meant to them to finally "get it." I took this opportunity to celebrate their success by giving them a special badge and announcing their accomplishment to the whole class.

The effect was immediate: the student beamed with pride, and their classmates cheered and congratulated them. It was a small gesture, but it made a big impact on the student's motivation and self-esteem. From that day on, they were even more motivated to continue learning and improving, and the class became even more supportive and encouraging.

This experience showed me the power of celebrating successes in gamification. By acknowledging and rewarding student achievements, we can boost their motivation and sense of accomplishment, which in turn can lead to even greater success and enjoyment in learning.

IT'S IMPORTANT TO NOT only provide regular feedback but also to celebrate successes along the way. Celebrating successes can help reinforce positive behavior and progress, and it can help create a sense of accomplishment and pride in students.

Set Up a Rewards System

One way to celebrate successes is to set up a rewards system. You can offer points, badges, or other prizes for achieving certain goals or milestones in the game. Make sure the rewards are meaningful and motivating for students.

Recognize Students Publicly

Another way to celebrate successes is to recognize students publicly. You can announce their achievements in class or display their progress on a leaderboard. This can help create a sense of healthy competition among students and motivate them to do their best.

Create a Celebration Event

Consider creating a special event to celebrate students' successes. This could be a pizza party, a game day, or another fun activity that students would enjoy. This can help create a sense of community and camaraderie among students, and it can help reinforce positive behavior and progress.

Provide Personalized Feedback

When celebrating successes, make sure to provide personalized feedback to each student. Acknowledge their specific achievements and the hard work they put in to get there. This can help create a sense of pride and accomplishment for each student.

Use Positive Language

When celebrating successes, make sure to use positive language. Avoid focusing on what students didn't do or haven't achieved yet. Instead, focus on the progress they've made and the positive behaviors they've exhibited.

Overall, celebrating successes is an important part of implementing gamification in the classroom. It can help reinforce positive behavior and progress, create a sense of accomplishment and pride in students, and motivate them to do their best.

Adjust as Needed

During the summer break, I had planned a gamified unit for my sixth-grade social studies class. I was excited about the different game mechanics I had chosen and how they would help to engage my students in the content. However, after the first few days, I noticed that some of my students were struggling with one of the game mechanics that involved completing research tasks in a limited amount of time.

Instead of ignoring the issue and pushing forward, I decided to adjust the game mechanics. I took some time to talk to my students and gather their feedback about the tasks and the time constraints. Based on their responses, I made some changes to the tasks and gave them more time to complete them.

This adjustment not only helped to increase student engagement but also improved the quality of their work. The students were able to better focus on the content without feeling rushed, and I was able to see their strengths and weaknesses more clearly. By being willing to adjust and make changes as needed, I was able to create a more effective and enjoyable learning experience for my students.

ADJUSTING YOUR GAMIFICATION strategy as needed is a crucial step in ensuring its success in the classroom. Even with careful planning, you may encounter unexpected challenges or discover that certain game mechanics are not working as well as you anticipated. This is where flexibility and adaptability come in.

First, regularly assess how the gamification is affecting student engagement and learning outcomes. You can do this through informal check-ins with students or more formal assessments, such as quizzes or surveys. Use this feedback to identify areas for improvement and to determine if any adjustments are necessary.

Next, be open to making changes to the game mechanics or rules as needed. This may involve adding or removing certain elements, adjusting point values, or modifying the way in which students earn rewards. When making changes, communicate clearly with your students and explain why you are making them. This can help maintain their buy-in and enthusiasm for the game.

Finally, don't be afraid to try new things. Gamification is a relatively new concept in education, and there is still much to be learned about what works best for different types of learners and subject areas. Be willing to experiment and take risks, and be open to feedback from students and colleagues. By being flexible and open-minded, you can continually refine and improve your gamification strategy to better meet the needs of your students.

Remember, gamification is meant to be a fun and engaging way to enhance learning, so don't be too rigid or rigidly attached to your original plan. Adjusting as needed can help ensure that your gamification efforts remain fresh and effective over time.

Chapter 4: Gamification Case Studies

IN THIS CHAPTER, WE will explore a variety of case studies that showcase the successful implementation of gamification in the classroom.

Case Study #1: The Epic Win

An English language teacher named Maria wanted to find a way to engage her students and make learning English more fun. She decided to use gamification to create an app that would help her students learn English in a fun and interactive way.

Maria began by defining her objectives for the app. She wanted to create an app that would help her students learn English vocabulary and grammar in a way that was engaging and interactive.

Next, she identified her audience: English language learners who were struggling with vocabulary and grammar.

Then, Maria chose her game mechanics, including points and badges, as well as a leaderboard to track student progress.

Maria then planned the content of the app, including a variety of interactive exercises and quizzes to reinforce English vocabulary and grammar concepts.

Once the app was developed, Maria introduced the concept to her students, setting clear expectations and providing regular feedback to keep them engaged and motivated.

As a result, her students became more engaged in learning English and began to make more progress in their studies. Maria celebrated their successes by recognizing them in front of the class and awarding badges and other rewards.

Over time, Maria adjusted the app based on student feedback and performance, making it even more engaging and effective.

By using game mechanics to create an interactive and engaging learning experience, Maria was able to help her students learn English more effectively and enjoyably.

Case Study #2: The Gamified Classroom

A high school science teacher named Mrs. Jackson implemented gamification in her classroom to increase student engagement and motivation. Mrs. Jackson noticed that her students were often disinterested in the material and struggled to retain information. She decided to introduce gamification as a way to make the content more interesting and interactive.

To do this, Mrs. Jackson used a platform called Classcraft, which allowed her to turn her class into a role-playing game. Students were able to create their own avatars and were placed in teams, each with their own unique strengths and weaknesses. The goal was for each team to work together to complete quests and earn points.

Mrs. Jackson also incorporated game elements into her lessons, such as unlocking achievements for completing assignments and earning badges for mastering certain skills. She also used leaderboards to track student progress and provide motivation for students to earn more points.

As a result of this gamification approach, Mrs. Jackson noticed a significant increase in student engagement and motivation. Students were more excited about coming to class and were actively participating in discussions and group work. Mrs. Jackson also saw an improvement in student retention and test scores.

One student in particular, named Hannah, struggled with science and was often disengaged in class. However, after the implementation of gamification, Hannah became one of the most active participants in the game and was eager to complete quests and earn points for her team. Her grades and test scores also showed improvement.

Overall, Mrs. Jackson found that gamification was an effective way to increase student engagement and motivation in her high school science class.

Case Study #3: The Flipped Classroom

A college professor found that the use of gamification helped to improve student performance in his flipped classroom approach to instruction. Students were more focused and invested in their learning, and they were able to apply what they learned in class to real-world situations.

The professor preferred the flipped classroom approach because it allowed for more personalized learning. Students could go back and review course material as many times as they needed, and the professor could provide individualized feedback to each student.

One unexpected benefit of adding gamification elements was the creation of a sense of community among the students. As they worked together to complete challenges and earn points, they began to form study groups and help each other with course material.

Overall, the use of gamification in the flipped classroom proved to be highly effective in engaging students and improving learning outcomes. The professor plans to continue using this approach in future classes and to explore new ways to incorporate gamification into his teaching.

Additionally, the professor noticed that the gamification aspect helped to create a sense of healthy competition among the students, which further motivated them to engage with the course materials.

One of the key benefits of the flipped classroom was that it allowed the professor to spend more time interacting with students during class time, rather than simply lecturing. This meant that the professor was able to provide more personalized support and feedback to each student, which helped to enhance their learning experience even further.

As a result of the success of the combination of gamification and a flipped classroom, the professor continued to use this method in subsequent semesters. He also shared his experience and best practices with colleagues, who were interested in implementing similar approaches in their own classrooms.

These case studies illustrate the power of gamification in the classroom. By introducing game mechanics and incentives, teachers can create a more engaging and motivating learning environment. While gamification may not be suitable for every subject or classroom, it is certainly worth considering as a way to improve student outcomes and create a more enjoyable learning experience.

Chapter 5: Measuring Success

Back when I was a student, I always loved participating in competitions. I remember one year, my English teacher decided to introduce a gamification element to our class by setting up a writing competition. We were divided into teams, and each team had to come up with a creative story within a set timeframe.

The teacher provided us with clear instructions and guidelines, and we were encouraged to use our creativity and imagination to come up with the best story possible. We worked tirelessly on our stories, collaborating and brainstorming together to create something truly unique.

At the end of the competition, the teacher announced the winning team, and they were rewarded with a prize. But the real reward was the satisfaction of knowing that we had all worked together to achieve something great. The competition had motivated us to put in extra effort and work harder, resulting in a higher level of engagement and interest in the subject. It was a great example of how gamification can be used to enhance the learning experience and encourage student success.

GAMIFICATION CAN BE a powerful tool for enhancing learning and engagement in the classroom. However, to truly evaluate its effectiveness, it is important to measure its impact.

In this chapter, we will explore various methods for measuring success in gamification, including:

- Quantitative measures
- Qualitative measures
- Surveys and feedback
- Analytics and data tracking

Quantitative Measures

Quantitative measures involve using numerical data to evaluate the success of gamification. This can include metrics such as:

- **Participation Rates:** How many students are actively engaging with the gamified activities?

- **Completion Rates:** How many students are successfully completing the challenges and quizzes?

- **Time Spent:** How much time are students spending on the gamified activities compared to traditional learning activities?

- **Grades and Test Scores:** Are students performing better academically as a result of the gamification?

Qualitative Measures

Qualitative measures involve collecting non-numerical data, such as feedback and observations, to evaluate the success of gamification. This can include methods such as:

- **Focus Groups**: Gathering a small group of students to discuss their experiences with the gamification.

- **Observations:** Observing students during gamified activities to see how they are engaging with the material.

- **Interviews:** Conducting one-on-one interviews with students to gather their feedback on the gamification.

Surveys and Feedback

Surveys and feedback can be a valuable tool for measuring success in gamification. This can include creating surveys for students to provide feedback on their experiences, as well as using feedback mechanisms within the gamified activities themselves to gather real-time feedback.

Analytics and Data Tracking

Analytics and data tracking involve collecting and analyzing data on student engagement and performance within the gamified activities. This can include using learning management system (LMS) analytics, as well as tracking data on specific game mechanics such as completion rates and time spent.

By utilizing these methods for measuring success, educators can gain a deeper understanding of the effectiveness of gamification in their classrooms. This information can then be used to refine and improve gamification strategies for even greater engagement and learning outcomes.

Chapter 6: Future Directions

GAMIFICATION IS A RAPIDLY growing field, and there are many exciting new developments on the horizon. In this chapter, we will explore some of the potential future directions for gamification in education.

Virtual and Augmented Reality

As virtual and augmented reality technologies continue to improve, they will become more accessible to educators. These immersive experiences have the potential to transform the learning experience, allowing students to explore concepts in a more interactive and engaging way. In a virtual or augmented reality environment, students can take part in simulations and role-playing scenarios, which can help them to understand complex concepts more deeply.

Artificial Intelligence

Artificial intelligence is already being used in many areas of education, and it has the potential to revolutionize gamification as well. By analyzing student data and providing personalized feedback, AI algorithms can create a more tailored learning experience. AI can also be used to create more sophisticated game mechanics, such as dynamic difficulty adjustment, which can keep students engaged and challenged.

Social and Collaborative Learning

As online and blended learning become more common, there is an increasing need for social and collaborative learning experiences. Gamification can be a powerful tool for promoting collaboration and teamwork. Multiplayer games and group challenges can foster a sense of community and engagement among students, and can help to develop important social skills.

Personalization

Finally, as gamification continues to evolve, there will be an increasing emphasis on personalization. By tailoring the learning experience to the needs and interests of individual students, educators can create a more engaging and effective learning environment. Personalization can be achieved through the use of adaptive learning technologies, which adjust the difficulty level and content of the game to match the individual learner's abilities and interests.

Virtual and Augmented Reality

I always found science class to be a bit of a struggle, but that all changed when my Biology 11 teacher introduced a new virtual reality (VR) learning program in class. We were given VR headsets and were able to explore the human body in a completely immersive way. We could see the different organs and systems in detail, and even manipulate them to see how they worked. It was like nothing I had ever experienced before in a classroom.

The VR program was not only engaging and fun, but it also helped me better understand the material. The interactive nature of the program made it easier to remember and apply what I learned in class. I also found that I was more motivated to study the material outside of class, because I was excited to see what other VR experiences my teacher had in store for us. The introduction of VR technology truly transformed my science education, and I can only imagine the impact it will have on education in the years to come.

VIRTUAL AND AUGMENTED reality (VR/AR) are quickly becoming popular in education, and they have the potential to transform the way we approach gamification. Gamification in education has always relied on engaging students through interactive and immersive experiences, and VR/AR technology takes this to the next level.

One of the biggest benefits of VR/AR is the ability to create realistic and immersive learning environments. For example, a history class could use VR to take students on a virtual tour of ancient ruins, allowing them to experience history firsthand. A biology class could use AR to overlay virtual images of organisms onto real-life specimens, enhancing the learning experience.

Another way VR/AR can impact gamification is by enhancing the game mechanics themselves. Imagine a VR escape room that requires students to solve math problems to progress through the room. Or an AR scavenger hunt that requires students to find and scan QR codes to reveal clues to a mystery.

The potential for VR/AR in gamification is virtually limitless, and as the technology becomes more accessible, we can expect to see more and more innovative uses in education. However, it is important to remember that not all schools and students have access to these technologies, and it is crucial to ensure that the benefits of gamification are available to all students, regardless of their access to technology.

Artificial Intelligence

As an educator, I have always wanted to personalize my lessons to meet the unique needs and interests of each student. With the help of artificial intelligence, I have been able to achieve this goal in a way that was never before possible.

Using an AI-powered gamification platform, I can create custom learning paths for each student based on their individual strengths, weaknesses, and preferences. The platform analyzes data on student performance and behavior to generate personalized recommendations for activities, challenges, and rewards.

For example, one of my students was struggling with multiplication tables. With the help of AI, I was able to create a customized game that focused on those specific areas. The game adjusted in real-time as the student progressed, providing additional support when needed and challenging them to reach their full potential.

Not only has AI helped me create more personalized learning experiences for my students, but it has also saved me time and energy by automating many of the administrative tasks associated with tracking student progress and providing feedback. Overall, I am excited to see how AI will continue to revolutionize the way we approach gamification in education.

ARTIFICIAL INTELLIGENCE (AI) is an emerging technology that has the potential to revolutionize gamification in education. With the ability to analyze vast amounts of data, AI can provide personalized learning experiences that adapt to the needs and preferences of individual students.

One application of AI in gamification is the use of intelligent tutoring systems (ITS). These systems use machine learning algorithms to analyze student performance data and provide feedback and personalized recommendations to improve learning outcomes.

Another application of AI in gamification is the use of chatbots as virtual teaching assistants. Chatbots can provide immediate feedback and answer questions from students, freeing up teachers' time to focus on more complex tasks.

AI can also be used to create more immersive and interactive gamification experiences. For example, AI-powered virtual environments can simulate real-world scenarios and enable students to practice skills and concepts in a safe and engaging way.

However, there are also potential challenges and ethical considerations associated with the use of AI in gamification. For example, there may be concerns about data privacy and bias in algorithmic decision-making.

Overall, AI has the potential to enhance gamification in education by providing personalized learning experiences, improving feedback and support, and creating more engaging and interactive learning environments. As the technology continues to evolve, it will be important to consider the potential benefits and risks associated with its use in gamification.

Social and Collaborative Learning

One of the things I had been struggling with in my English Literature class was how to get my students to work together more effectively. One day, I decided to introduce a gamified project that required them to collaborate in groups. I noticed that some students were hesitant to work with others, so I decided to add a social element to the project.

I introduced a leaderboard that tracked each group's progress, but also added a social element where students could earn bonus points for helping each other. I also set up a discussion forum where students could ask questions and share ideas.

To my surprise, the social and collaborative elements of the project led to a huge increase in engagement and motivation. Students who were previously hesitant to work with others were now actively seeking out help and feedback from their peers. They were also more invested in their group's success, since they knew it would impact their own score on the leaderboard.

The social and collaborative learning aspect of gamification proved to be a powerful motivator for my students, and it made me realize the potential of incorporating these elements into future lessons and projects.

GAMIFICATION IN EDUCATION has already shown great potential in enhancing engagement and motivation among students. However, with the growing emphasis on social and collaborative learning, gamification is set to become an even more powerful tool for educational purposes.

Social and collaborative learning refer to the processes of sharing knowledge and skills among students, either through working together in groups or through peer-to-peer learning. These processes are highly effective, as they encourage active participation and engagement among students, and can lead to deeper learning and better retention of information.

Gamification can greatly enhance social and collaborative learning by providing a framework for students to work together and collaborate on learning activities. For example, gamified learning activities can be designed to encourage peer-to-peer teaching, where students teach each other through interactive quizzes, group projects, or collaborative problem-solving tasks.

Gamification can also create a sense of friendly competition and teamwork among students, which can lead to increased motivation and engagement. Leaderboards, badges, and other gamification elements can be used to encourage students to work together and achieve shared goals.

In addition, gamification can provide a way to monitor and assess the progress of social and collaborative learning activities. By using gamification metrics and analytics, teachers can track the performance of individual students and groups, identify areas for improvement, and provide personalized feedback and support.

Overall, social and collaborative learning combined with gamification can create a highly engaging and effective learning environment that promotes active participation, teamwork, and deep learning.

Personalization

One of my worst memories from school is math class. For years I struggled with concepts and often felt lost during lessons. I dreaded math assignments and tests, and my grades suffered as a result. Then, one year, my teacher introduced a new gamified math program that incorporated personalization.

The program analyzed my strengths and weaknesses, and created a personalized learning path for me. The program included various game mechanics, such as points, badges, and leaderboards, which motivated me to keep going. I could see my progress and felt encouraged to continue working on the areas where I needed improvement.

The program also allowed me to work at my own pace and gave me instant feedback, which helped me correct my mistakes right away. I felt like I was in control of my learning and could see the impact of my efforts.

Thanks to the gamified math program, I not only improved my math skills, but also gained confidence in my abilities. I no longer feared math class and actually looked forward to tackling new concepts. Personalization in gamification made a huge difference in my learning experience.

GAMIFICATION HAS BEEN a buzzword in education for some time now, and it's easy to see why. It's an effective way to engage and motivate students, while also helping them learn in a fun and interactive way. But as technology advances, the possibilities for gamification in education are expanding even further. One area that's particularly promising is personalization.

Personalization involves tailoring the learning experience to the individual needs and preferences of each student. This can be done in a variety of ways, from adapting the difficulty level of a game to match the student's abilities, to creating custom learning paths that address their specific interests.

In the context of gamification, personalization can take many forms. For example, a teacher might create different challenges or quests for each student based on their interests and learning needs. Or, a game might adapt to the student's performance, providing hints or extra challenges as needed.

One of the most exciting aspects of personalization in gamification is the potential for data-driven decision making. By analyzing data on each student's performance and preferences, teachers and game designers can gain insights into what works and what doesn't. This information can then be used to further refine and tailor the learning experience for each individual student.

Another benefit of personalization in gamification is its potential to promote self-directed learning. By allowing students to take control of their own learning, and providing them with personalized feedback and guidance, they can develop a sense of ownership over their education. This can help to foster a love of learning that will serve them well throughout their lives.

Overall, personalization is set to have a major impact on gamification in education. As technology continues to advance, we can expect to see even more exciting developments in this area.

In conclusion, the future of gamification in education is bright, with many exciting new developments on the horizon. By staying up-to-date with the latest trends and technologies, educators can continue to harness the power of gamification to create engaging and effective learning experiences for their students.

Conclusion

As I looked out at the sea of faces in my classroom, I felt a sense of pride and satisfaction. I had implemented gamification in my classroom and had seen the positive impact it had on my students. They were more engaged, motivated, and excited about learning.

One of my students, a quiet and reserved girl, had approached me after class to tell me how much she enjoyed the game-based learning activities we had been doing. She said that it made her feel like she was playing a fun game, but at the same time, she was learning new things and challenging herself.

Another student, who had previously struggled in my class, had shown a significant improvement in his grades and was now participating more actively in class discussions. He said that the game-based approach made learning more enjoyable for him, and he found it easier to focus on the material.

As I reflected on my experience, I realized that gamification had not only made learning more engaging and fun for my students but had also helped me become a better teacher. It had challenged me to think outside the box and come up with creative ways to make learning more meaningful and relevant for my students.

Overall, I was convinced that gamification had a powerful impact on education and had the potential to transform the way we teach and learn. As I closed the door to my classroom, I couldn't help but feel excited about the future possibilities of gamification in education.

———————————

GAMIFICATION HAS THE potential to transform education by creating engaging and interactive learning experiences that promote student motivation, achievement, and retention. By incorporating game elements such as points, badges, and leaderboards into educational activities, gamification can make learning more fun and meaningful for students.

In this book, we have explored the key concepts and strategies involved in gamification, from defining objectives and identifying audiences to choosing game mechanics and planning content. We have also discussed the importance of introducing the concept, setting clear expectations, providing regular feedback, celebrating successes, and adjusting as needed.

We have examined several case studies that illustrate the effectiveness of gamification in diverse educational settings, from elementary schools to colleges. These case studies have shown that gamification can improve student engagement, motivation, and learning outcomes.

As technology continues to evolve, gamification is also evolving. The rise of virtual and augmented reality, artificial intelligence, social and collaborative learning, and personalization are just a few examples of how gamification is adapting to meet the changing needs of students and educators.

In the future, gamification will continue to play a crucial role in education, as it has the potential to create more personalized and interactive learning experiences that cater to the unique needs and interests of individual learners. However, it is important to remember that gamification is not a silver bullet and should not be viewed as a substitute for effective teaching practices.

Ultimately, the success of gamification in education will depend on the willingness of educators to embrace it and integrate it into their teaching practices in a thoughtful and intentional way. By doing so, they can create more engaging and effective learning experiences that help students achieve their full potential.

Further Reading

KAPP, KARL. *The Gamification of Learning and Instruction: Game-based Methods and Strategies for Training and Education.* John Wiley & Sons, 2012.

Kapp, Karl, and Lucas Blair. *The Gamification of Learning and Instruction Fieldbook: Ideas into Practice.* John Wiley & Sons, 2013.

Kim, Sangkyun, et al. *Gamification in Learning and Education: Enjoy Learning Like Gaming.* Springer, 2018.

Matera, Michael. *Explore Like a Pirate: Engage, Enrich, and Elevate Your Learners with Gamification and Game-inspired Course Design.* Dave Burgess Consulting, Inc., 2015.

Don't miss out!

Visit the website below and you can sign up to receive emails whenever Cheryl Angst publishes a new book. There's no charge and no obligation.

https://books2read.com/r/B-A-SBAY-SKCIC

BOOKS2READ

Connecting independent readers to independent writers.

About the Author

Cheryl Angst has been teaching in the classroom for over twenty-five years. With a Masters in curriculum and instruction, her passion centers around finding tips, tricks, and strategies to enhance her practice.

Cheryl is a firm believer that learning should be fun for both the students and the teacher. If it isn't engaging, or doesn't spark joy, it's likely able to be done differently.

The "Quick Reads for Busy Educators" series is designed to maximize the precious time educators have. Each book is short enough to be read in an hour or less, but contains a wealth of information on the topic. Some books are overviews of strategies and approaches (enough to help educators decide if it's for them) and some are deeper dives into specific aspects of those larger approaches. This allows busy educators to grab the information they need quickly and efficiently.

If there's a topic you'd like to see covered in the "Quick Reads" series, please let us know!